T0198896

INSPIRATIONAL
POEMS

Build Up The Soul

John Wehrspann

AuthorHouse™
1663 Liberty Drive
Bloomington, IN 47403
www.authorhouse.com
Phone: 1 (800) 839-8640

Because of the dynamic nature of the Internet, any web addresses or links contained in this book may have changed since publication and may no longer be valid. The views expressed in this work are solely those of the author and do not necessarily reflect the views of the publisher, and the publisher hereby disclaims any responsibility for them.

This book is printed on acid-free paper.

ISBN: 978-1-7283-5844-4 (sc)
ISBN: 978-1-7283-5843-7 (e)

Library of Congress Control Number: 2020906374

Print information available on the last page.

Published by AuthorHouse 04/09/2020

authorHOUSE®

BEAUTIFUL

As I awaken in the early morning
Your beauty takes my breath away

I can feel my heart melt
With so much love for you

You are the center of my
World and I would
Do anything for you
My love

CALMING

As I sat looking into the sky listening to
what nature had to say so early in the morning.

You could hear the doves singing after a good rain shown
and the ground was damp from the early morning shower.

The birds seemed to come alive as I sat
looking into the sky ever so quiet and listening
to the early morning singing from nature all around me.

The clouds seemed to move ever so slowly
as time seemed to fly by on this calming morning.

It was so stimulating as I sat listening to nature singing
so early in this beautiful morning.

So as you sit and listen to the calming of
nature look into the sky and forget time.

CAMPING

As I sit outside the camper
I can hear the birds chirping
I find the water calming
as I watch the river flowing

As I sit outside the camper
I watch the ducks diving in the water
All upon the morning dew

As I sit outside the camper
I hear all the fellow campers
Arising to a new day

As I sit outside my camper
I sip my morning coffee and wonder
Why more people don't do this to relax

As you sit outside your camper
What would you doing?

CAT

Pets are family to
Like a cat named Jeffery
A big orange cat that warms
The hearts of anyone he is close to

A Friend and companion
He is there through thick and thin
What ever life dishes out
He will be there for you

Were ever I go he goes
When I am hurting and
Need someone to talk to
He is there for me

Jeffery more then a cat
A true best friend
One whom never puts
You down or hurt you

Pets make you feel good
And they listen so well
And sometimes you swear
They understand what you say

CHILLING

The chill of a morning frost
chills you to the bone and
you shiver from the cold

This chill is like a feeling
of anger and frustration
it can also chill you to the bone

As the coldness brought on a chill it
can eat away at your soul
you feel this anger and frustration
Building and eating away at you
It can also chill you to the bone

Look to the positive side of life
It will help you smile and warm
you from the inside out

CHURCH

The building stood with all its pride
As weather hammered it
The sun rained down on it

The building stood with all its greatness
With all its colored glass
Red bricks white windows

The building stood with all Gods blessing
The church drew me within
The warmth and welcome
Made the building stand

EARLY MORNING RAIN

The smell of an early morning rain
Feels refreshing to the senses

As the rain pitters-patters on the
Roof tops it has a hypnotic sense over you

As the sky shows its true colors
of a rain bow the rain has
refreshed the earth

As you catch this aw of
God you feel blest as he
has refreshed your soul
to start a new

FEELING

With my arms rapped around you
I can feel our hearts beat in rhythm
we can dance to the rhythm in our hearts

with the feel of your body
close to mine makes me feel
like floating on the clouds
close to heaven and God

upon looking to the heavens
white fluffy clouds floating
I think of you my love

the bible states, God created
man and woman to become one
with you I am complete
God indented us to become one

INTERNAL FIRE

As my internal fire burns for you
my heart beats faster and faster.

As my internal fire burns with passion
I feel my soul being won over with your love.

As my internal fire burns with desire
I feel myself being drawn closer and closer into your heart.

As my internal fire burn my emotions
come flooding outward and shows
the softness within my heart, the passion within
my soul and my desire being drawn for into your heart.

JEEP

As I jumped into the jeep
with the top lowered
to allow for the suns raises
With all its glory to rain down on me

As I driving the sun shining
I could feel the gentle breeze
blow threw my hair

As I turned the radio up loud
I was lost in how beautiful the
Day was

LOVE

Insecurity is a bad feeling
The ugliness of it is questioning
everything and everyone around you

insecurity is you are not sure were
you stand in a relationship
so the question keeps popping up
"Are we good baby?"

We should have more faith in ourselves
know as long as we love ourselves
others will follow and love us also

LOVER'S MOON

As I stepped out into the darkness my fate was lit by a lover's moon.

As it was full and bright the ring that engulfed the
lover's moon glowed like silvery ring.

As I stood admiring the site and to know that Tammy my
true love was gazing upon the lover's moon.

As we admired this wonder of the lover's moon I
knew it was fate that brought us together.

As two of us period into the bright light of the lover's moon my day became
brighter as my love grew for you Tammy my angel grew stronger.

As not to stumble or falter from the path our love
will grew stronger as time goes on.

MEANING OF LOVE

As I look deep into your eyes my heart
Begins to melt with such a deep love.

As I take hold of your hand
I can feel my soul reaching out for you.

As I lean in for a kiss
My heart, soul and spirit become one with you.

As we become one in heart, soul and spirit
We find true meaning of love everlasting

MORNING BEAUTY

Wake in the morning and turn over
looking into the face of a beautiful women
the one whom you love so much with all your heart
your heart flatters with such deep love

As her eyes open and your eyes meet
the sparkle in her eyes melts your heart
you place a genital kiss upon her lips

the waking of this early morning
bring a sparkle in your day
you feel yourself melting
In her beauty

MORNING GLOW

Looking over the horizon we could
see the trees and all their glory

The leafs all different colors
the birds singing in the tree tops

The sun peaking through the clouds
then in a blink of an eye the sun shone
over the tree tops giving a holy glow to the trees

we felt a glow over our hearts for each other
and she takes my breath way I look at her
her beauty and it takes my breath away

she is a very glowing person whom my breath
is taken away by her beauty and
has captured my heart

15

MOTHER

A mother is a woman whom
God made perfect in everyway

A mother is a woman whom
Take care of man threw all
Their bumps and bruises along
The way and backs tem through
Life without question

A mother is a woman whom bares
Children and takes all the pain
And punishment that is put on
Her body but still looks beautiful
For all to see and shine with well being

A mother is a woman whom helps
Her children threw life all the
Hardships school boyfriends or girlfriends
With care and lifts them up when ever they are down

A mother is a woman whom all
God children takes for granted
So, when you investigate your
Mother face thank God for
Her for she is your saver in life give
Her all the love you can
Because were would you be without your mother from God

PAIN

Pain takes your breath away
when ever you try and move

Pain makes you want to cry
pain hurts so bad and you
can't just make it go away

Pain pulls you down you
must remain still because
the pain is intense

Pain makes you feel like
you take advantage of loved
ones

PAINT

God created us in his image no matter the color on the paper

We go through life trying to change how we look by
removing the color we are on the inside

But no matter what you do to change your appearing the painted
color shines through so why change whom you are and except it

An artist always starts with a clear canvas and then lays out his art

God did this when he made us you can't change
the canvas by just repainting yourself

Be leave in yourself and how you look never worry what
others may know we were all made in Gods image

So we are all painted perfect and should never have to change how we look
Love yourself for god created you perfect

PASSION

lying next to you
Our body temperature rises
We feel the passion for each other

Lying here in your arms
Is like being in heaven
you would never let go

Loving you is all I want to do
Stay here never leaving your side
even if the world is passing us by

POOL SIDE DREAMS

As the sun shone onto the pool the ripples on the pool glistened
you find yourself being lost into the ripples of the water

As you stare at the ripples of the water the sun made it sparkle and you find
yourselves day dreaming, and all your problem drifted away into the ripples

As laughter of children playing you can you feel yourselves
playing with them as though you are young again

Where would you drift off to in the moment in time as you sit
watching the sparkling ripples on the water in the pool

RELATIONSHIP

Here is a woman who is like me
Love her with all my heart
She makes me feel like a real man

She is a woman who knows what
She wants in life and is not afraid
To tell you what she thinks

In my eyes she is perfect
I can be who I am and
She loves me for it that
Is a true relationship

SOUL MATE

As I look deep into your eyes
I can see deep into your soul
Your heart is full of happy and joy

As I look deep into your eyes
I can see deep into your soul
You are full of love and affection

As I look deep into your eyes
I can see deep into your soul
And see your true feelings towards me

As I look deep into your eyes
I can see deep into your soul
And see that you feel as I do
And we have such a strong love for
Each other

As I look deep into your eyes
I can see how you melt in my arms
As I lean into kiss your lips
We become one soul

As I look deep into your eyes
I make love to you I get
Lost in your soul and I
Never want to be found

Loving you is in my heart and soul
And it will stay forever and never leave

SPECIAL BIRTHDAY

The day in which you were born
You brought hope to a young couple
They looked to God and prayed for you

The day in which you were born
You brought happiness
to this young couple and the world

The day in which you were born
You brought joy
to this young couple and the world

The day in which you were born
You brought love
to this young couple and the world

The day in which you were born
Is your special birthday
to this young couple and the world

You are a very special person
The world and everyone in it
Wish you all the hope, happiness, joy and love

THE FLIGHT OF A DOVE

The measure of love is like a dove
taking flight for the first time.

A dove waits for the hand of God
to lift them to the heavens.

So does our hearts it waits for the
hand of God to lift it to the heavens.

So when we feel love for each other look
to the heavens for those doves being
lifted by the hand of God.

As the dove takes to the heavens they go
with your heart as God lifts them up to the
heavens.

THE FLIGHT OF AN EAGLE

The eagle opens its wings and
falls into the wind and is carried away
on the flow of he/she takes flight

As we watch from the ground we can only imagine
what this would feel like to find the
true meaning of a free spirit

The eagle glides high into
the heavens and looks down
on everything and everyone
Below

He can feel so free nothing
to restricted him in flight

He is as light as a feather floating
on water and not even a ripple in the water
as the feather just floats away

THE SUNSET BEACH

Laying on the beach watching the sun set
lying close to you feeling your smooth body
next to mine as the warm sand beneath the
blanket keeps use all toasty and warm

As the sun starts to set and the sun seems
to sink into the ocean its glow bounces off
the water and gleams through your hair

I can feel myself being drawn closer and closer
to you with my heart beating faster and faster
with all my heart and soul

I feel all my emotions flooding out of me
and hold you ever so gently in my arms
with loving affections that I just let myself go

So as the sun disappeared and the moon arose
we made love under the moon light with
made passionate love.

Workday

The starting of a work week
You arise and now its back
To work

You ponder over your bills
And think how to pay them
For the month

You ponder over can you
Afford gas for the week

You ponder if you have
Enough money for work
You ponder over every
Little thing until it engulfs
You with stress

As we arise for work
We should just focus
In what a beautiful day
Outside it is and laugh
Off the bills and the daily
Events.

Printed in the United States
By Bookmasters